SHOUT TO THE LORD WHEN YOU CAN'T SHOUT

SHOUT TO THE LORD WHEN YOU CAN'T SHOUT

By

Glen Dunnam

E-BookTime, LLC
Montgomery, Alabama

SHOUT TO THE LORD
WHEN YOU CAN'T SHOUT

Copyright © 2005 by Glen Dunnam

All rights reserved. No part of this book may be reproduced or transmitted in any form or by any means, electronic or mechanical, including photocopying, recording, or by any information storage and retrieval system, without permission in writing from the copyright owner.

ISBN: 1-59824-053-6

First Edition
Published July 2005
E-BookTime, LLC
6598 Pumpkin Road
Montgomery, AL 36108
www.e-booktime.com

Contents

Foreword 7

Introduction 9

Chapter 1 Shout to the Lord 11

Chapter 2 What do you do when everything goes wrong? 13

Chapter 3 Don't Be Afraid! Only Believe! 15

Chapter 4 Do you "conquer" or "be conquered?" 17

Chapter 5 Let God's "revelation" take over your situation. 20

Chapter 6 God takes your "negatives" and makes them "positives." 23

Chapter 7 Let your faith arise! 28

Chapter 8 The Journey of Recovery 30

Chapter 9 How do you deal with the things you have been dealt? 33

Chapter 10 Let the Redeemed of the Lord say so! 37

**Shout To The Lord
When You Can't Shout**

Foreword

It has been my distinct privilege to serve as Glen & Michele Dunnam's Pastor for the past ten years. Not only have they been faithful parishioners, but also dear friends. I have watched as God has taken the Dunnams on a journey that has produced a tremendous spiritual maturation in their lives. Through good and sometimes very difficult circumstances this couple has demonstrated the truth that all things do work together for good to those who love God and are called according to his purpose. This book tells one of the stories in the Dunnam's lives. It is written from a heartfelt conviction that as this human drama unfolds you will be encouraged to believe God for the impossible in your life. God has proven himself faithful to Glen and Michele and as you read this book, my prayer is that you will discover and know the loving concern and care that God has for you. God bless you, Glen and Michele, and may this book bless many people as God reveals himself in its pages as the God of the miraculous.

Mike Glover
First Assembly of God
Jonesboro, Arkansas

Shout To The Lord
When You Can't Shout

Introduction

On Monday, December 1, 1986, Glen Dunnam almost lost his life in a "three-wheeler" accident. While rabbit hunting, Glen was riding his three-wheeler when an unseen half-inch steel cable that was stretched across the road hit his neck. The cable nearly decapitated him, severing his trachea, esophagus and the nerves leading to his voice box. Miraculously, his jugular veins and spinal cord were undamaged. His rapid recovery baffled the doctors who said his recovery was indeed "miraculous."

Isn't it an awesome thought that the God of our universe can and will take time to reach down and intervene in our life situations? This true-life account of the miraculous survival and recovery in Glen's life is a wonderful reminder of how a deep experience and personal relationship with God can take us through the most challenging seasons in life. 2 Timothy 4:2 reminds us to be "ready in season and out of season". We need to be prepared at any time, whether convenient or inconvenient, to proclaim God's word and patiently instruct those who may not understand or even accept it. The personal testimonies of those who witnessed this awesome intervention by the Lord will show that even at an "inconvenient" time, Glen was sure to give the "thumbs-up" that everything would be okay because God was in charge.

It blesses me to be married to this wonderful man and watch his spiritual walk and intimate relationship with the Lord grow daily. He is truly a priceless gift from God. Our family is thankful to the Lord for allowing us to have him here with us today. As we walk through each season of our life together, I am reminded that: God knows the plans He has for us-plans to prosper and not harm us-plans to give us a hope and a future. (Jeremiah 29:11) What an awesome thought!

>I love you sweetheart!
>Michele Dunnam

**Shout To The Lord
When You Can't Shout**

Chapter 1

Shout to the Lord

Psalm 37:4 says *"Delight yourself also in the Lord and He shall give you the desires of your heart."* I knew as a small child, that the Lord had His hand upon my life. Remembering the days of my youth, I look back and see how God was directing my path.

My uncle and aunt taught children's church for about twenty years. They were a huge part of my influence in the ministry. I saw a hunger and desire in them, to serve the Lord with all their heart, soul, and strength. As they taught children, I saw a zeal for the Lord that I wanted. My uncle would let me be involved in various parts of the services. One Sunday, he let me share a Bible story with the children. From that day on, I knew that somehow I would be in ministry.

I began teaching more and more as the Lord opened doors. I would dress up as characters, and teach with puppets. The more I would give of myself, the more I wanted to minister.

The Lord blessed me with two Christian friends, the best that anyone could ask for, to grow up with. We had a lot of fun together and enjoyed sharing the gospel with each other. Some adults have accountability partners or friends. While growing up we held each other accountable to live the way God wanted us to live. These guys helped me to grow close to God. I went from childhood to adulthood with the trust to believe God for whatever I faced. God was training us at a young age to have a love and hunger for God and His work.

I also had several youth pastors as a teenager. My first youth pastor was a man of wisdom. He saw the call of God on my life. I remember him letting me preach my first sermon. I really knocked them out! I read from Matthew 7:7, *"Knock and it shall be opened, seek and you will find."* You know the scripture. All I could do was read the scripture. At the ripe old age of twelve, I was ready to throw in the towel. I remember how embarrassing it was not being able to say anything else. Thank God for men and women of aged wisdom. My youth pastor put his arm around me and in front of everyone told them how proud he was of me. I didn't know it then, but he was planting a seed deep down inside of me. Little did I know that someday, I would be in the same position as youth pastor he was in.

Later, in my teen years, I experienced some things I was not quite ready for. These were "TRIALS." I thought you got into the ministry, and never had any more problems. Guess what? I was wrong! I found out that God was going to take me on the ride of my life. The trials I was facing caused me to turn to the Lord. Sure, there was plenty of opportunity to turn to the things of this world (alcohol, drugs, and sex). But I felt like Peter did in Matthew 5:68, *"But Lord, who would we go to?"*

God blessed me with a Sr. Pastor that taught the Word with authority- the authority to walk on top of your problems, instead of letting your problems walk over you. By this time, we also had another youth pastor that played a major part in my life and influenced me in ministry as well. God was preparing me for His work all the time. There were many days I wondered what was going on and if I was going to make it. But thank God, He is the Alpha and Omega. He knows the beginning, and He will be there to the end. God taught me through life's difficult experiences to stay focused on Him. In youth service, my youth pastor taught me how to stand firm on the word of God, and his wife taught the word to me as my Sunday school teacher. They both had faith in me, that I could make it through any trial that came my way. I thank God for men and women, who know how to impart the word, faith, love and confidence, into people's lives. We need to learn how to be like Christ, in that we love people, instead of judging. We never know what kind of maturing process they're going through.

Shout To The Lord When You Can't Shout

Chapter 2

What do you do when everything goes wrong?

Hollywood has a way of portraying a fantasy world to us, that of life without any problems. It's a kind of a "Leave it to Beaver" complex. This sounds really good, but it's not true.

Jesus suffered many things. He went through rejection, pain, loss, physical and verbal abuse, yet He was the Son of God. What makes us think we are not going to go through trials? Trials are to mature us to become what God's plan is for our life, and to show forth His Glory and His power, to deliver us in time of need. I Peter 4:12-13 says, *"Beloved, do not think it strange concerning the fiery trial which is to try you, as though some strange thing happened to you: but rejoice, to the extent that you partake of Christ's sufferings, that when His glory is revealed, you may also be glad with exceeding joy."* "God wants to take us from mountaintop to mountaintop. The only problem is, between the two mountains, there is a valley that has to be traveled. In the valley is where God restores my soul. This is where we find plenty of spring water to drink, and a lot of fruit and vegetables to eat. Why? Because in the valley it is green and productive. Also, in the valley, lying in wait for a meal, are all wild animals. We can't just run into the valley or we will be eaten alive. Psalm 23 teaches us that we have to be led by our Great Shepherd. The Shepherd has walked the path before us and knows the danger that lies ahead. Our Shepherd

Glen Dunnam

knows how to guide us through the valley. He knows when to stop, "He makes me to lie down in green pastures" and when to go, "He leads me beside still waters", You can be assured that you are going to go through the valley, but you are not going through it alone. Your Great Shepherd "Jesus Christ" is going with you. He knows the way through the valley and He's not afraid of the wild beasts that wait there. The Lord has already defeated them before us. We have to follow His direction, and correction in our lives.

When you feel like running away because of the valley experience, remember that the Great Shepherd is guiding you to the next mountaintop.

Shout To The Lord
When You Can't Shout

Chapter 3

Don't Be Afraid! Only Believe!

I was twenty-four years old when I began to fulfill the role as youth pastor in the same church I grew up in. I did all the things a youth pastor was supposed to do. Within a one hundred-mile radius, I took the young people to every theme park, bowling alley, mall, horseback riding, camping, and lock-in available. It was a lot of fun, but fun was not all I wanted the young people to experience. While growing up, I'd had an experience with the move of God in my life that I wanted them to experience. I wasn't satisfied with just playing games, and running myself ragged. God began to deal with me about fasting and prayer. I asked the young people to join me on a three day fast. To my surprise, several of them made it through the full three days. After this fasting period, God honored the youth's step of faith. God began to touch the lives of the young people in a great way. They were stepping out in faith, and declaring the word of the Lord. The Lord was saving and touching their lives at a rapid pace. It sounds great to say that God is moving in a mighty way, but there will always be a hellish opposition to the move of God. Little did I know about what was going to happen in my life personally. In the story of Job, Satan got in the face of God, and God picked a fight with him. He said, "Have you considered my servant Job?" God knew exactly how Job would respond to the trials of life. You see, God had already kicked Satan out of heaven, and He defeated him once again. Job was a winner. He was an overcomer and victorious, before he ever lost the first family member or piece of property. The trial I was about to face was not faced alone. Just like Job, God made me a conqueror before it ever started. God instructed me from the word of God in Mark 5:36, *"Don't be afraid; only believe."* This particular story is of Jairus, who had a 12-year-old daughter that had been sick unto death. He went to find Jesus and asked Him to come and heal his daughter. Jesus went with him but He was not in a hurry. In the meantime, He stopped and healed another lady on the way. By this time, one of the servants came from Jairus' house and told him the worst news any parent could hear. "Don't bother Jesus any further, for your daughter is dead." Jesus could see the hopelessness in Jairus' face, and said these words, "Don't be afraid, only believe." Jesus is still saying these words to us today. Your situation may seem hopeless, but in Christ, all things are possible.

Shout To The Lord When You Can't Shout

Chapter 4

Do you "conquer" or "be conquered?"

Thanksgiving Holiday was upon us in 1986. The church, where I served as youth pastor, had a private school in which I also worked. The Wednesday before Thanksgiving, I was wishing the students a happy and safe holiday. I told them all to be very safe so they could come back to school the next week. Prior to this, one of our young men had called to talk about some situations in his life. The bottom line is, he needed the Lord. He accepted Jesus as Savior, that day in my car. He told me that he liked to hunt, as did I. We planned a hunting trip the Monday following Thanksgiving. This is where our journey begins.

On December 1, 1986, at approximately 10:00 a.m., I was on a hunting expedition with this young man from my youth group. I had a 185 Honda three wheeler on which we left to go rabbit hunting. I had traveled these field roads many times. My three-year-old son had ridden with me days prior to this trip. As we were traveling down the road, I was telling the young man about a couple that lived close to where we were going to hunt. The couple attended our church too. They were both employed at our local community college. She was about seven and a half months pregnant. I later found out that she had stayed home that particular day for a doctor's appointment. I lived in Blytheville Arkansas then. It was an average town of thirty thousand people and included a local airbase facility.

Glen Dunnam

Blytheville had a local hospital, but it was not equipped for trauma situations. The closest trauma unit, "The Elvis Presley Trauma Center" was in Memphis, Tennessee, about eighty miles away.

That day was a turning point for me. We were traveling down this old abandoned county road at about ten to fifteen miles an hour. It was a misty, cloudy morning and I pointed out to the young man where the couple lived. We were at a crossroad getting ready to turn, when suddenly I caught something in the corner of my eye. A farmer had strung up a half-inch steel cable across the old road to keep 4x4 trucks from destroying his field. It was lying very low and not flagged. The cable caught the front wheel of the three-wheeler and stretched it out like a rubber band. On the cycle, I had a gun sock and had squeezed two 12-gauge shotguns inside it. The cable slid up the cycle's wheel, and up the gun sock. Then it broke one of the gunstocks and cracked the other. The cable came above the guns and struck me in the neck, knocking us both off the three-wheeler.

I got up and felt of my neck realizing that something was wrong. I began running to the only house in the area within a mile. It was about 100 yards away. About halfway, as I was running toward the house, I remembered the young man that was with me. I looked back and he was standing up. I was trying to tell him to come on, but I couldn't talk loudly.

Not knowing what kind of damage had occurred, I began to claim God's Word. I remembered that if I honored my mother and father, that God would honor me with long life. I knew that I was not going to die. When we reached the house, we weren't sure if anyone would be home. But God had already set the battle plan in motion. The enemy thought he was sneaking up on God while He wasn't looking, but God had set strategic people in place. The expectant mother had stayed home for a doctor's appointment scheduled for later that morning. We all got into the young lady's car, and began our emergency travel to the hospital, which was about ten miles away. Let me remind you, that the hospital was not equipped to take care of this kind of trauma. But again, God had His plan set into motion. With injuries to the neck, you need at least two doctors for sure. The doctors needed would be a general surgeon, and ear, nose, and throat doctor. The odds of having both doctors there at the same time were not very

Shout To The Lord
When You Can't Shout

high. In addition, it was a miracle an operating room was open for a non-scheduled surgery.

God once again, showed His power to intervene on behalf of His children. As we pulled up to the emergency entrance, the two doctors that were needed had just stepped out of surgery. The ER staff began working with me and immediately noticed the lack of oxygen. At that time I was transferred to the operating room for surgery. God was making us more than conquerors!

Chapter 5

Let God's "revelation" take over your situation.

When the cable hit my throat, it scratched the outside of my neck, just like when you were a child and fell down and scraped your knee or elbow. But the x-rays revealed that the cable had caused more damage than that. The doctors told my family that nearly everything in my neck had been completely severed. During the surgical procedure, the doctors did an emergency tracheotomy to stabilize my breathing. X-rays revealed that the trachea (windpipe) and esophagus (food tube) had been completely severed, along with the nerves leading to the voice box. The doctors opened my neck from side to side. The ear, nose, and throat doctors had to reach inside my chest cavity to pull up my trachea. They then sewed it to the side of my neck to prevent it from falling back into my chest cavity.

They placed a trachea breathing tube in my throat. The only things that were not damaged were my jugular veins and my spine. During the process of getting to the hospital and going through surgery, my lungs filled up with fluid. Blytheville doctors and staff had done all they could do. Because it was a cloudy day, the Life-Flight could not fly to Blytheville to transport me to the Elvis Presley Trauma Center. I was going to be moved by ambulance, to Memphis, which was an hour and ten minutes away.

Shout To The Lord
When You Can't Shout

Before I left the hospital, the doctors told my family that I would be very lucky if I made it out of the city limits because of the fluid in my lungs. The "revelation" my family had to face was devastating. In times of great trial and stress, we must believe "God's revelation". That "revelation" is that God's promises will stand taller than our situations. The doctors were saying that I was going to die, but God's word was saying, "that with long life would I satisfy you."

My uncle is a man of great faith. He told me later that he asked the doctor what the situation looked like. The doctor told him that I would probably not make it out of town. But, my uncle knew the "revelation", and did not look at the situation. He told the doctor that I would live and not die. He also said that I would speak again.

From that point on, God began performing miracles, one after another. Needless to say, I did make it to the trauma unit in Memphis. I arrived there at about 12:30 p.m. by ambulance. When I got there, they immediately began observing me. By 1:15 p.m., my family had arrived. The doctors in Memphis had already looked at the x-rays from the hospital in Blytheville. They noticed that my lungs were full of fluid. That's when they began taking their own x-rays. It took about three hours for them to observe and x-ray me. It was about 4:15 p.m. before they came out and consulted with my family.

Now hold on to your hats and pull up your stockings because you are going to hear how God began to perform miracles in my life. I want to remind you of the young people just a few pages back. By this time, the ER waiting room was filled with about fifty young people joining hands and praying for their youth pastor. The enemy wants to kill, steal, and destroy. He will do whatever it takes to do just that. You see, God had anointed me to be the leader, or "head" of the youth group. What better way to stop what God was doing than by cutting off the "head" of leadership? He thought if he could shut my mouth, the young people would die spiritually.

What a mistake he made! That group of young people began to call on God and rebuked the enemy with "authority"! These young men and women had been fasting and praying and had already seen God move in a mighty way. They knew this situation was not too difficult for God to handle, because of the "revelation" of God's word in their lives. As the doctors began to look at their own x-rays, they revealed to my family, the extent of the injuries. The results, none of which were good, were numerous. This is what the doctors said:

1. My esophagus (food tube) and trachea (windpipe) had been completely transected.

2. The vocal cords nerves had been completely severed.

3. They could not tell if there had been any damage to the spine. If there was, it could cause paralysis.

4. Because the esophagus was so fragile, there was a possibility it would have to be left undone for surgery at a later date.

5. The fluid on my lungs could require surgery, and cause the lungs to collapse, which would result in opening the chest. There would be a very high risk of not living through surgery.

6. The voice box would probably have to be removed.

7. I would have to be hospitalized for minimum of six months.

8. There would be multiple surgeries involved over the next several months.

9. I would never speak again.

10. It would be a minimum of a two-year recovery.

Shout To The Lord
When You Can't Shout

Chapter 6

God takes your "negatives" and makes them "positives."

God had every step ordered from the time I got up that morning. I was accustomed to fasting two or three days a week and this particular day was one of those days. As you are well aware, the night before you go into any kind of surgery you have to go on an "NPO" diet, meaning no food or drink after midnight. If I had eaten or drank anything, they could not have performed surgery without complications. Let me just take time here to share a little bit of the word of God. God's word says, "He will never leave us or forsake us." Hebrew 13:5. Everything the surgeons had to say was "negative". But our "negative" reports are God's opportunity to bring a "positive" report and victory into our lives. As I told you previously, the x-rays from Blytheville had shown that my lungs were filled with fluid. The Elvis Presley Trauma Center, also known as "The Med" had taken their own x-rays. To their surprise, the x-rays revealed different results from those the Blytheville hospital had forwarded. God began to perform miracles on my behalf. Let me share with you the "negatives", that God turned into "positives".

- The fluid that was in my lungs had moved into my stomach. This was a miracle within itself.

- My blood pressure and heart rate had remained stable through out the observation period.

- The surgeons were able to repair and reconnect both the esophagus and the trachea during surgery.

- They did not remove the voice box.

- After two days I no longer needed the respirator.

- On the third day, I was moved to a step down ICU unit. (Minimum stay in Trauma "was" to be 2-3 weeks).

- Two days later I was moved to a private room.

- On December 11, 1986, I spoke for the first time. The doctor did not have an explanation for my ability to speak.

- On December 12, 1986, I had complete respiratory arrest. Only minutes from death, God intervened once again.

God continued to perform miracles, one after another. Each time I needed God to move on my behalf, contact would be made to my home church. They would have special prayer on Sunday, and by Monday morning God had answered their prayers. The church prayed a simple prayer. They would turn and face toward Memphis saying, "Do it Lord". Each time, He did it! As I remember what God performed, I hope it blesses you as much as it blesses me! After all the initial surgeries were completed they moved me to the trauma ICU. I'm not sure how long it was before I knew exactly where I was, but, I remember a nurse waking me up, asking my name and if I knew what had happened to me. I shook my head yes, unable to talk.

There were many doctors and interns, which would come in to observe, and discuss the situation. The Assistant Professor of Surgery, Saade S. Mahfood, M.D., was one of the surgeons that assisted in my surgery. He came to my bedside in the trauma unit and I asked him a question with my hands. I raised my hand in a puppet motion, asking him if I would ever talk again. Dr. Mahfood was very blunt and straightforward. He said that I would never speak

Shout To The Lord
When You Can't Shout

another word in my life. I could not speak at all, but when Dr. Mahfood said that, I replied with my hands. I pointed to heaven saying that I would speak again. He shook his head "no". When my family would come into the ICU unit, I couldn't speak to them with my voice. But, I would stick both of my thumbs up, as if to say that everything was going to be all right. God had given me the assurance that He had everything under control.

A few days later I was moved to a private room. I had lost a tremendous amount of weight. Again, my church prayed and within one week, I gained six to eight pounds. On December 11th, I felt like I could actually take a deep breath for the first time since the day of my accident. I inhaled and it felt so good to take such a deep breath. The next time I did it, I tried to speak. To my surprise, I spoke for the first time! The words that came out of my mouth were those of praise. I told the Lord that I loved Him. I was so excited when I spoke! I just had to tell someone.

With some assistance in dialing the phone, I called my mom in Blytheville. Mom had a special way of answering the phone. She was always full of joy and zeal, proud that anyone would call. If she were a tele-marketer, you would buy ten of whatever she was selling! While the phone was ringing, I knew she was going to be excited to hear from me.

Mom picked up the phone, and answered it in her usual way. But that day was different. She answered, and as I said, "Hello Mom", she began crying, unable to speak. She handed the phone to my sister, who began shouting! All I wanted to do was to talk to someone! Finally, they gained their composure and I got to talk to them. God is so good! The next morning was a morning I wasn't expecting, following the excitement of the previous day. I woke up at about 5:00 a.m. finding it very difficult to breathe through my trachea tube. I paged the nurse to come to my room and wrote a note explaining that it was hard to breathe. She started to suction the mucus from the trachea and during the process, my airway completely closed off. She instructed me to raise my arms up. At that time, I passed out on the bed, and went into convulsions. I later learned that she had called a "Code Blue".

Immediately, a team of doctors and nurses were in my room working to save my life. Maybe you have heard of what is called N.D.E. or Near Death Experience. During this time of rescue, I remember traveling through a dark tunnel going upward. I was crying out to God asking, "God where are You"? The third time I cried out, I was in the most beautiful, bright light I had ever seen. I didn't see heaven, or Jesus. However, the peace that I experienced was overwhelming. The only way I can explain it is if you took all the cares of this world and could fix them immediately, that was the peace that I felt.

During this NDE, it was as if I was at the top of my hospital room watching the doctors and nurses working on my body. God spoke to me in my own country boy way. You see my Mom and Dad would tell us kids that everything was going to be okay. This was their way of saying that they were going to take care of it. God spoke to me in this experience and told me that "everything was going to be alright."

As I was leaving that place of peace, both of my hands were raised in praise to God. When I was revived, both of my hands were in the air praising God, just like I was while in that perfect place of peace. God just kept intervening everyday in my life. Even in the surgical procedure in which the doctors wired my jaws, God was with me! They pushed a wire through my jaws, between my teeth, going down to my collarbones. The reason for the wires was so I would not pull anything apart that the doctors had sewn together in my neck. They also put drain tubes in both sides of my neck. When I would try to drink anything, it would go down my throat, and drain out the sides of my neck. The doctors said that before the wires could come out of my jaws, the drainage would have to completely stop.

Again the church family was contacted. They stood and turned toward Memphis and said, "Do it Lord!" The next week drainage had completely stopped. The next two weeks I was able to maintain a liquid diet and gain a considerable amount of weight. On December 24th I was released from the hospital. Before I left the hospital the doctors tried to plug off my trachea tube to see how well I would do breathing through my mouth and nose. It didn't take long for my breathing to become labored and they unplugged the tube. The doctor told me that if it didn't get any better, I would have to live with the trachea tube forever. I replied to him, that as sure I was sitting in

Shout To The Lord
When You Can't Shout

front of him, there would be a day I would meet him again without a trachea tube.

Previously, the doctors had told me it would be at least a six-month stay in the hospital. Here I was, going home after three weeks and two days. This was the best Christmas present I had ever received. Praise God for His power that can intervene in our lives! You can let God turn all your negatives into positives if you only believe.

Chapter 7

Let your faith arise!

I couldn't wait to go to back to church. My church family had stood, prayed, and believed God for miracles. December 27th 1986, was my first Sunday back at church. I will never forget that day. I had already spoken with my pastor, and told him that I didn't need a lot of physical contact due to everything I had been through. My head tilted downward because my jaws had been wired down. It took about three months for my neck to relax enough to straighten up. My pastor had instructed me to come in late that Sunday and come right on up to the platform. When I walked into the service, there were hundreds of people there. They had heard that I was going to be there to share the miracles God had performed in my life.

As I was walking down the aisle of the church, the congregation began standing and applauding as I was making my way to the platform. When I got to the platform everyone was praising God for what He had done. My pastor talked just for a few moments, and handed the microphone to me. At this time, I still had a trachea tube in my throat in order to breathe. The way I spoke was by taking a deep breath of air, and putting my finger over the trachea tube. This caused the air to come out of my mouth and nose. I shared all that God had done for me and how every time they prayed, God had answered their prayers. Faith was building in their hearts. There were many needs that morning in the lives of the people of God. The same

Shout To The Lord
When You Can't Shout

God that performed the miracles in my life was about to perform miracles in that service.

As I finished sharing all God had done in my life, our pastor called for people who had needs in their lives. First he called for those who needed the Lord, and several came down to receive Christ as Lord and Savior. Then he called for those who were sick in their body. Many came to the altar and were healed. There was a couple that brought their child down for prayer because the doctors had told them that his legs were growing crooked. Doctors had said that he would need to wear braces on his legs. God intervened and healed him and the doctors later confirmed that he was not going to need braces. Another man could not walk without a cane or some type of assistance. He couldn't walk up stairs at all. Our platform had ten to twelve steps to climb in order to reach the top. When God healed this man, he not only walked without a cane, but also climbed the stairs without any assistance.

A dear sister had suffered from severe sinus congestion for weeks. She had been to the doctors several times and had not gotten any relief. She was instantly healed. The pain and congestion immediately disappeared. God performed many more miracles that day, not because of me, but because the church had exercised their faith, and dared to believe God.

Chapter 8

The Journey of Recovery

After the holidays I began my road to recovery. I came home with a trachea tube in my throat. The trachea tube had to be taken out everyday to be cleaned. This procedure was not easy to do. However, in order to come home, I had to learn this.

I was making trips to Memphis once a week for checkups. On January 5th, the doctors told me the tracheotomy would be a permanent part of my life. I was determined to prove them wrong. I began covering up the breathing tube with a piece of tape. I would go all day with my trachea tube completely closed off. At nighttime, I would uncover it, "so I wouldn't wake up dead." Everything was going good except for one thing. My esophagus was building up scar tissue and was hindering my ability to swallow. In the afternoon, it would relax and open enough for me to swallow some soup. I didn't want to go back to the hospital, so I went several weeks unable to eat enough food to maintain a proper diet.

The doctor was concerned and tried to dilate my throat in an outpatient procedure. They tried twice, neither being successful.

March 13, 1987, I was again hospitalized because of the restriction in my esophagus. The doctors tried to dilate my throat and were unsuccessful. They told me it would take major surgery to correct the problem. They would open my stomach, take part of my intestine and

Shout To The Lord
When You Can't Shout

put it in my throat. Instead of having one scar, I would have two. Unfortunately, there would be no guarantee that it would work properly. Before they could do anything, my body had to be replenished and built up with vitamins and nutrients. I had lost so much weight and was very weak physically. They could not do surgery for several weeks. That was the last bit of news I wanted to hear. I was already weak physically and emotionally.

The doctors told me that I would be in the hospital for at least four more weeks. I wasn't prepared to stay for that length of time. So I asked for a two-hour pass to go home and get the things I needed. I cried from the time that I left the hospital until I returned. When I got back I thought, "God, I can't do this again!" I went to sleep that night feeling very depressed. But God is so good to His children! His promise is that He will never leave us, nor forsake us. The next morning I woke up not feeling much better. I was mentally and emotionally exhausted. I couldn't understand why God was allowing this after all the miracles He had already performed.

I know that some of you have it all together and you never ask the question "why?" That particular day I was asking "why." About seven o'clock that morning, a nurse came into my room. I had not seen this nurse before. She was doing her daily routine of checking the charts and greeting the patients. She looked at my chart and said "Good Morning Mr. Dunnam." I have to be honest with you, I was not very friendly because of the emotional state I was in. I said good morning back to her, but was not very convincing that it was indeed a good morning. God will always be on time when we need Him. I definitely needed Him that morning. She continued looking at my chart and said something that caught my attention. She started by saying, "I'm not sure you are going to understand me. But I was at church last night." When she said that, my ears perked up. All "antennas" were receiving messages to listen up! She said that while she was singing a song in church the previous night, the Lord spoke to her about coming to my room number. He instructed her to sing a song. She began to sing the words of this song. "I sing because I'm happy, I sing because I'm free, His eyes are on the sparrow and I know He watches me." As she finished the song she said, "Mr. Dunnam, God told me to tell you that His eyes are upon you." God is an "on time" God, yes He is! He may not come when you want Him, but He'll be there right on time. He's an "on time" God, yes, He is. When the nurse finished speaking what God had told her to say to me, I told her she would never know what she had done for me that day.

After she left my room, I felt like I could run through a troop and leap over a wall. I didn't know exactly what I was to face in the weeks to come. All I knew was that God was going to walk with me through whatever I would face. The doctors first put an I.V. in the main artery of my chest to build up my immune system. It also caused me to gain weight. Two weeks later, one of the doctors came in and had me swallow a lead fishing weight with a fishing line connected to it! It was a day I'll never forget. This was to be a guideline for the dilator to slide down my throat and stretch the scar tissue. They tried several times but were unsuccessful. Dr. Saade Mahfood came to my room and said that he had never seen an esophagus he could not dilate.

The next morning, he took me into surgery and told me he would attempt to dilate my esophagus first. If this procedure did not work, then they would continue with surgery. Before I went into surgery I was carrying a cup with me to spit in. I could not even swallow my own saliva. When I awoke from the anesthesia, the first thing I did was try swallowing. To my surprise, I could feel my saliva going all the way down to my stomach. I was excited and began clapping my hands. The nurses in the recovery room thought I was having problems. They didn't know that I'd not had anything to eat or drink in weeks. The doctor had been able to dilate my esophagus without any further surgery. I went from being unable to eat or drink to, within three days, enjoying whatever I wanted to eat and drink. God was continuing to perform miracles in the midst of all situations. God's eyes were truly on me, just as they are on the sparrow.

On April 5th 1987, I was dismissed from the hospital with instructions to use the dilator four to six time a day. I had to learn to dilate my esophagus by swallowing an eighteen-inch long dilator about the diameter of a garden hose. I would swallow this four to six times a day in order to be able to eat normally. I have been eating normally ever since. April 22, 1987 the tracheotomy was removed and I resumed normal breathing. Since then I have spoken at several churches and have been invited on TV programs. God has allowed me to go through a trying time in my life to mature, and to show Satan that he is defeated in my life!

Shout To The Lord
When You Can't Shout

Chapter 9

How do you deal with the things you have been dealt?

The things God did for me in those months were unbelievable. The excitement of miracle after miracle was faith building for both the church and me. I thank God for the voice He has created in me and praise Him for His mighty power. The voice you hear is a miracle because it is impossible to speak with severed, paralyzed vocal cords! But I also went through some times of great stress and depression. Depression is not a bad thing, but is the result of substantial loss in our lives. We learn how to deal with our depression by grieving. It is God's way within ourselves, to help us through difficult times. For the first year after my accident, all I had was a whisper to speak with. I was thankful for that. However, you have to understand my call and vocation was to preach and share the word of God. I tried to preach a few times after my accident and had a difficult time trying to talk and breathe. It was very frustrating wanting to share God's word but lacking the ability to share it with the excitement felt inside. There were several times that I threw my Bible in the corner and said that I would not preach again. The emotions I went through were a mix of ups and downs. One day I felt like I could jump over a wall and the next day I felt like the wall had fallen on me.

During this time in my life, I had two small sons. I was worried about not being able to talk to them. I wanted to teach them about life, and

Glen Dunnam

share with them the things that I had learned. I felt like they were not going to be able to hear me. I had to train them to respond to my clap, or whistle. If I did either one of these, both of my boys would come running to see what I wanted. God gave them a special ear in which to hear my whistle and the understanding to come. I want to remind you of what the doctor had said regarding my tracheotomy when I was leaving the hospital on Christmas Eve. He said if my breathing didn't get any better, I would have to live with the trachea tube for the rest of my life. I told the doctor there would be a day I would see him again without the tracheotomy.

Two years after my accident I was in our local Kroger store buying groceries. I caught something green in the corner of my eye. After being in the hospital for a long time, my eyes got used to seeing the green scrubs the interns wore. I looked down the aisle and to my surprise there was the doctor that said I would probably never get rid of my tube. So I walked up to him and said, "Do you remember me?" He looked at me for a second and said, "Yes I do." I reminded him of our conversation in the hospital 2 years before, when I told him I would speak to him one day without a tracheotomy. This would be that day!

I love the Lord with all my heart, and love to go to church. My entire life I have enjoyed the presence of the Lord. I have always expressed my love for the Lord in an emotional and verbal way. After my accident I couldn't verbally praise the Lord with a loud voice. As a child I had learned how to whistle loudly. I couldn't shout to the Lord, so I whistled to Him. The word says, "Make a joyful noise unto the Lord." When I went to church everyone else would sing and praise the Lord, and I would whistle and praise the Lord.

About a year and a half later, my voice began getting louder and stronger. I had shared my testimony in many churches and Christian schools in the surrounding area. It took about six months to fully realize the miracle God had actually done in my life. I was in the doctor's office looking at the other patients. Many of them were talking with only a whisper. There I sat with a tremendous amount of damage to my throat and voice box, but with a louder voice than any of them. Another day I was at my uncle's lawn mower shop, when he called me over to meet someone. The gentleman got close to my ear and whispered, "I don't want you to get discouraged. I read an article

Shout To The Lord
When You Can't Shout

in Reader's Digest about a doctor who can inject something behind one vocal cord to pull them closer together and make our voices louder. When I find out about this I will call you." I looked at the man and said, "Thank you. I would appreciate that." My voice was ten times louder than his was. Amazed, he wanted to know what I did to make my voice so loud. I began telling him of the miracles God had done for me.

While riding a four-wheeler, he had run into a fence causing damage to his chest. The doctors had to do an emergency tracheotomy to save his life. In the process they hit one of the nerves to his vocal cords and damaged it. He had one vocal cord paralyzed and one that was not. I had all the nerves cut to my vocal cords and both cords are paralyzed, but my voice was louder than his was. Now, eighteen years later, both of my cords are still paralyzed. However, my voice continues to be strong. Praise God for His miracles in my life!

When I had my trachea tube removed, the doctor told me that if by chance one of the vocal cords moved to a different position, it could restrict my airway. In that case, someone or myself would have to cut my throat and reinsert the trachea tube. The only complications I have are when I get a sore throat, then my vocal cords swell, restricting my airway. On a September morning in 1996, I woke up with a terribly sore throat. It was one of those sore throats that feels like you swallowed a porcupine. I was trying to soothe it with a hot cup of coffee, but that was a big mistake. If you have a swollen knee or ankle you put an ice pack on it to reduce the swelling. If you put heat on it, the heat will cause the blood flow to increase in that area causing even more swelling. After drinking the hot coffee, my airway began closing off. I was breathing a little when suddenly there was nothing. My family called 9-1-1 and the paramedics were there in a matter of minutes. Before they got there I remembered what the doctor had told me about possibly reinserting the trachea tube in an emergency. I had the old tube from ten years before. I used it in sharing my testimony. I grabbed a razor blade and the trachea tube from my closet. Then I stood in front of my bathroom mirror, took the razor blade and cut my throat where the old trachea scar was. I cut once through the skin, and then the second time through the trachea. After that, I placed the same trachea tube back in my throat from ten years earlier. I spent 4 days in the hospital and had a brief bout with pneumonia after inhaling blood into my lungs. The self-tracheotomy, no doubt, saved my life. I had to go back to my ENT doctor to determine what repairs would be necessary to once again be free of the trachea tube. The vocal cords are in a V-shape. At the bottom of the cords, there is a joint much like the bend in your finger, which opens and closes the vocal cords. The doctors had discussed doing a laser surgery on one of those joints that would cause the vocal cord to pull over to one side giving a wider airway. He said that in doing the surgery, I would lose what voice I had.

The only options I had were to do the surgery, or live with the tracheotomy the rest of my life. I knew I would not be happy with the tracheotomy. My boys and I enjoyed swimming and canoeing. There would be no way we could do those activities with a trachea tube. As I contemplated the options, I decided that whispering would not be the worst thing in life. So I opted for surgery. The morning of the surgery, I was waiting in my room for the personnel to come and get me. The phone rang and I answered it. It was the doctor calling from the operating room. He told me that he was not going to do the surgery we had discussed. The day before, he had been on the phone talking to other doctors around the nation about my case. There was one doctor in West Virginia who had a patient with a similar situation. Instead of the laser surgery on the joint of the vocal cord, he cut a V-shape out of one of the cords causing a larger airway. The results were going to be the same, but not as damaging to the throat. The doctor said I would still come out with only a whisper. However, after the surgery my voice sounded the same as before. The doctor said my voice was loud because of the swelling from surgery. He also told me that after the swelling went down, my voice would gradually go away. But instead of getting lower and quieter, my voice stayed amazingly the same volume as before. It was another time God took the negative and made a positive in my life.

About eight weeks later the doctors once again removed the tracheotomy from my throat. I have been trachea tube free ever since. I am now forty-five years young and sharing what God has done for me anywhere the opportunity opens.

Chapter 10

Let the Redeemed of the Lord say so!

I want to share with you some of the personal statements and testimonies of my family members and church family as they were given the report of my condition at the hospital. They have shared their response to what the doctors said, and what was their most faith building experience through out the accident and recovery period.

Nina James, my aunt

The doctors said it would be very doubtful you would make it to Memphis. My response to the doctor's report was that, "You don't know the God I know AND the God that Glen knows." The most faith building experience for me was your attitude and the way your faith held out when really and truly, we didn't know if you were going to make it or not. When we would visit you, there was a gleem in your eye and you would stick up your thumbs as if to say, "Everything was going to be alright." That would build my faith when my faith was real low. When your faith was low we just kept believing God because your work wasn't done.

Roger Sloan, church family

As you were being transported from Blytheville to the trauma center, I spoke to a personal friend who was a nurse at the Elvis Presley Trauma Center. She was able to contact the ambulance in route to the trauma unit. After she spoke to the paramedics, she told me that things did not look good. I was told that you had a very traumatic injury to your vocal cords and windpipe and that you were not responding at that time. The outcome didn't look very good and it was very, very serious. Not really knowing what had happened in the accident, I did not accept the report I was hearing. I had known you for a long time and I knew how strong your faith was. I believed God had a bigger calling on your life and that God would intervene. The most faith building thing for me was being able to realize that no matter what trials we go through and regardless of the negative reports, we have faith in a stronger power with the ability to overcome. I believe that God is in charge of any circumstance, big or small.

Shout To The Lord
When You Can't Shout

Johnny Ray, Church Family

I was told that the prognosis was really bad and you were in critical condition. The doctor that had done the emergency tracheotomy in Blytheville was responsible for keeping you alive and getting you to the Med. When I heard the doctors report I was scared to death. The most faith building part was when we would hear the news from the medical profession and then see God respond to their news. The church would hear a need in your life and every service they would turn toward Memphis and pray this simple prayer, "Do it Lord." And God would do it.

Beverly Ray, Church Family

The day of your accident I heard that you had practically decapitated yourself and there wasn't much hope that you were going to survive it. My response to the doctor's reports was that they are not always the same as God's reports. The most faith building part to me was that every negative report that came from the doctor, God simply reversed. It was also faith building that our children didn't just hear about what God could do. They witnessed for themselves what God could do!

Shout To The Lord
When You Can't Shout

Dr. Terri Brassfield, cousin, Asst. Pastor

By the time Ken and I got to the hospital they had already loaded you up in the ambulance and were getting ready to take you to Memphis. The word was for us to be prepared that you would not make it to Memphis. Then I looked at Ken and said, "We won't believe that report and we'll not accept it! But he will make it to Memphis and God will do a miracle." I believe the most faith building part to me was your faith during the whole process. That evening they let us see you for a few seconds and you looked towards us and stuck both thumbs up. I knew that if you could hang in there and press on, this thing was going to be all right.

Loyd Dunnam, Dad

I didn't really know anything at first until Mom and I got to the hospital in Memphis. Then we knew the news was bad. I remember when mom and I came to your room after you got out of surgery and you stuck your thumbs up at us. I believe that was the most faith building to me.

Shout To The Lord
When You Can't Shout

Brenda Folkner, E.R. Nurse / Friend

I remember they wheeled you in and I could hear that your breathing was restricted. We actually thought your trachea was crushed because we could hear that the air was not going through. We could see the thin line where the cable had hit your throat. Your color was really pale. The doctors had just stepped out of surgery and we had you in surgery in a matter of minutes. It was a miracle that they even had a room open for surgery. When the doctors tried to do the tracheotomy, the trachea was recessed down into your chest. After we later heard how much damage was done to you, we realized that it was a miracle that you even made it to the hospital. It just wasn't your time to go yet.

Tommie James Jr., Uncle

When they were putting you in the ambulance the doctor was standing there by you. I asked him how it was. He told me that it was bad and it would be a miracle if you made it out of town. I told him it WOULD be a miracle because you WERE going to make it. I feel like God was with you from the beginning. The Lord had a purpose for it from the beginning and He was going to use it for His glory. All things work together for the good for those who love Him.

Shout To The Lord
When You Can't Shout

Barry James, Cousin / Brother

The doctors said that if you lived, (and that was a very strong word "If"), then they would have to repair the airway. They said that you would never speak again. The outlook was very, very dim. I knew that you were a fighter and your faith in God was very strong. Your faith would pull you through no matter which way it went. The most faith building for me was when you almost died and the people locally and nationwide prayed. That is when God moved on the scene.

Ronnie Self, E.R. Paramedic

When you came into the hospital we didn't really know how serious the injuries were. I figured you were a dead man. I thought you would make it to Memphis, but I didn't think you would live.

Shout To The Lord
When You Can't Shout

Brenda Holifield, Youth Pastor, R.N.

When you got to the hospital you were in acute distress. The cable you hit had severed your trachea and esophagus. Their first priority was to maintain an airway. The doctors did an emergency tracheotomy. We stayed at the Med a long time that night with a lot of other church family. The doctors came out and told us all the repairs they had done. I knew that with you, and your determination and faith, everything else would come into place. The doctors said you would never speak or eat normally again. The totality of the accident was faith building. But the most faith building part to me was the evening I came down after you had stopped breathing. As they worked on saving your life, you told us how you were in the presence of God and watched them as they tried to revive you.

Billy Hollifield, Youth Pastor

I went back with the family to talk to the doctors. The doctors said that your nerves to the larynx were completely severed and you would never speak again. We began to pray and ask God to take care of you. The most faith building part to me was the morning that you literally died and came back to tell us about it. I knew that if you could go through that, then you would make it.

Shout To The Lord
When You Can't Shout

Diane Razer, Sister

The doctors said that you were in very bad shape and probably would not make it to Memphis. We were devastated at the news, but we knew God was big enough to take care of it. When we walked into the room that night you held your thumbs up as if to say that you were going to be all right. The most faith building part for me was the first Sunday you were at church. To see you walk into the church and down the aisle was wonderful. You were truly a walking miracle.

James Ray, Young man in the youth group

We heard that you were in a bad accident and were in pretty bad shape. The prognosis was not good at all. My response to the doctor's report first was shock. It went from shock to worry. It was really tough to know the shape you were in. The most faith building to me was two things. One was your miraculous recovery. Secondly, the unity of the young people and being focused on one thing. The church was united because of their faith. That resulted in miracles and testimonies from your accident. The young people became much stronger.

Shout To The Lord
When You Can't Shout

Enclosed is a copy of the letter I received from Saade S. Mahfood, M.D., a doctor from the University of Tennessee/Memphis

March 21, 1988

Dear Mr. Dunnam,

I have been involved in the care of Mr. Dunnam since December 1, 1986. While riding a three-wheeler, he struck a hidden wire across the anterior neck. He transferred from Blytheville Hospital following a tracheotomy. The thoracic and ENT services were involved in neck exploration procedures. The following operations were performed: A. Cervical tracheal anastomosis. B. Cervical Esophageal Debridement reanastomosis. C. Flexible bronchoscopy. D. Neck fixation in flexion. At the time of exploration, his trachea and esophagus were lacerated and transected. Mr. Dunnam made a remarkable recovery following these operations. On follow-up an esophageal stricture necessitated readmission to the hospital and dilatation under anesthesia. The patient was then instructed to perform self-dilatation. Initially this was done on a daily basis and recently on a weekly schedule. Mr. Dunnam is currently without complaints. He tolerates regular diet, has gained weight, his voice has changed since the accident, however, and he is able to converse fluently. I feel he will continue to improve his ability to use his voice in the future.

Mr. Dunnam has been discharged from our thoracic clinic and he is to return on an "as needed" basis. If I can be of any further assistance, please do not hesitate to contact this office.

> Sincerely,
> Saade S. Mahfood. M.D.
> Assistant Professor, Surgery

God took a situation the devil thought he had full control over, and used for his glory. No matter what is going on in your life, God is still bigger than what you're facing. God can still cause water to come out of the rock, and dry up the Red Sea in your life. He will cause you to walk on dry ground. The giant may look bigger than life, but it's not bigger than God. Whatever miracle you need in your life, "God can". In the end we are more than conquerors. The enemy thought that by taking all of Job's possessions, he would end up possessing him.

Glen Dunnam

Job's faith in God brought him through difficult times in his life. When everyone else is saying give up, you know in your heart God will "show up and show out". What do you do when you can't shout? You praise Him with whatever you have. It could be a clap, dance, or a whistle. The word tells us to make a joyful noise unto the Lord. Praise Ye the Lord!

Shout To The Lord
When You Can't Shout

Contact:

Glen & Michele Dunnam
1001 Paragould Drive
Jonesboro, AR 72401

glendunnam@sbcglobal.net

Phone 870-930-3842

Printed in the United States
34079LVS00005B/268-1014